The " Little Theatre " Series
Edited by John Hampden

PRELUDE TO BALLET

Prelude to Ballet

An Analysis

and a

Guide to Appreciation

by Arnold L. Haskell

With decorations by
M. Doboujinsky

Thomas Nelson & Sons Ltd
London   1936

First published, June 1936
Reprinted, August 1936; July 1938

TO

CLAUDIA AND BRUCE OTTLEY

SOUVENIR

OF SO MANY

BALLET OCCASIONS

I HAVE attempted here a practical guide to the appreciation of ballet as an art, with small parallel sections on its history and practice.

It is written from the point of view of the audience and I have tried to make it as objective and as general as possible. I have aired none of my pet theories, attached it to the work of no one particular company. In every case I have given actual examples drawn from ballets in current repertoires, the result of a long experience on both sides of the stage.

If it can add something to the enjoyment of a visit to the ballet, and so induce further visits, I shall be well satisfied. Three performances usually suffice to create a confirmed *balletomane*, who will (bank balance permitting) rush to book seats for the rest of the season.

ARNOLD L. HASKELL

CONTENTS

PRELUDE TO BALLET

ON THE NEED FOR CRITICAL STANDARDS

No form of theatrical art is more difficult to understand than ballet. To the person who has sat enthralled through an occasional performance marvelling every time a dancer rose on tiptoe this statement may well seem absurd.

At a performance by the de Basil Russian Ballet in Bournemouth, my neighbour, a dear old lady in a very remarkable hat, expressed her amazement that the dancers were making the same movements that night as they had the night before. She had imagined the whole thing to be a brilliant improvisation. She was, I think, a trifle disappointed and the dancers had definitely gone down in her estimation, 'though of course it *is* clever of them to remember exactly what to do'. She had learned her first lesson.

Perhaps hers is an extreme case, but there is very little to guide the layman. The play has its printed text, the concert its score, and the cinema, however much of a miracle, is but photography, a logical extension of snapping the children on the sea-shore with the No. 1 Brownie everyone possesses.

The ballet has its traditions and precedents which, like the British constitution, cannot be fully revealed between the covers of any book. To talk to the average *balletomane*, as the enthusiast is called, is to gain very little help. He has a jargon of his own, he refers to the dancers of the day by their Christian names and while he is certain to be fiercely partisan, all praise or blame for what he is watching that night, he will not tolerate a word of criticism from the out-sider. Consequently, more often than not his en-thusiasm has a totally contrary effect.

Since 1933 we have had so much ballet in England that would-be *balletomanes* have arisen by the hundred. They pay almost nightly visits to the theatre, are familiar with the gossip of the wings, and shout loudly when their favourites appear. Inevitably, the majority lack any critical standards, since they have learned through watching comparative beginners rather than finished artists. Any company depends a great deal on its regular public for the actual quality of the performances given. Pavlova herself once complained to the author that in whatever manner she performed her 'Swan', the applause was always the same.

It is essential therefore for the enthusiast to possess some kind of critical standard as a basis for true enjoyment, for to marvel at the dancer on tiptoe may give pleasure on the first occasion, but when it becomes familiar it will soon seem a rather unneces- sary proceeding, which in fact it is, taken away from its context.

.   .   .   .   .   .

How natural and effortless seem the movements of these sylphs as they flit to and fro in the moonlit glade. Surely they are not real, and we are dreaming them as we listen to the music. How tenderly he lifts her as she escapes from his grasp and floats up into the air and then floats down again, skimming the surface of the stage with her toes.

We are watching the first ballet on the programme *Les Sylphides*, most admirable of all, most delicate and difficult to produce.

Let us take it apart and examine it with care. Such familiarity cannot be vandalism when it teaches us to admire and understand its creators, to praise a good performance and to sorrow at a bad one.

At what are we looking? Sylphs? No; at people

like ourselves, trained as dancers, performing a certain sequence of steps. After a time we may notice them as individuals, pause to examine their physique, their technical proficiency, their ability to act, or in this case rather to suggest an atmosphere (one of the most difficult problems in all acting) and the manner in which they react to the music. We are also looking at the costumes, their form and colour against a painted background. We are looking at all these things, and at the same time listening to a symphony orchestra.

If this particular performance of *Les Sylphides* is that rare and exquisite thing, a perfect one, and we are seeing it for the first time, we shall certainly not be aware of any detail, only of the sum total, 'a romantic reverie'.[1] One jarring note alone would stand out and demand our attention, yet each one of these things contributes to this beautiful picture, as well as many others that are never seen or known, concealed behind the painted backcloth.

Ballet, like Opera, is a meeting-place of the arts, music, painting, drama, but, whereas on paper Opera appears to be an equally happy blend, in fact it often has grave flaws, for to find a singer with the

[1] Such is its official programme description.

voice of a Melba and the physique, grace and dramatic genius of a Pavlova combined is obviously almost an impossibility. Consequently, we have the daily spectacle of elephantine Butterflies, buxom and aggressively healthy Mimis claiming to be in the last throes of consumption and ponderous Venuses, all of whom inspire ridicule unless the eyes are tightly closed; an illogical proceeding in a theatre. Avoirdupois, not poor music, only too often ruins Opera. It is by combining with ballet, as in the famous Diaghileff production of *Le Coq d'Or* (Covent Garden, 1914), sung by the finest singers, standing in the wings, and mimed by the greatest dancers that complete harmony can be obtained. Yet, for years ballet has suffered through being considered the frivolous younger sister of the blue stocking opera, a sop to induce the tired business man to accompany his wife to Covent Garden. Opera apparently was improving, ballet an idle entertainment. It is only since the advent of Serge Diaghileff to Western Europe in 1909 that ballet began to be taken at all seriously and that the Russian attitude gained ground.

I propose in this small book to run over each one of the elements that compose ballet and to review them historically, aesthetically, and in practice. Nothing could be more confusing to write about. (This is not an attempt at an excuse, should the task prove too heavy.) The initial difficulty is to know in which order to begin, the age old problem, the chicken or the egg? In this case, the music, the drama, the picture or the movement? In practice, as we shall see, so closely are they interwoven that it is difficult to make any rule, but for the purpose of clarity some order must be found, however arbitrary.

II

THE DANCER AS APPRENTICE:
SYLPHIDE–CHRYSALIS STAGE

T HE dancer seems the most logical person with whom to commence, since it is in dancing that the arts composing ballet unite.

For complete understanding the first place to meet the dancer is not on the stage disguised by make-up, costume and excitement, but in the classroom, where as a small child she is struggling, red-faced and perspiring, with some problem of motion or equilibrium. Her mouth set, her damp hair sleeked back and secured in a net or loosely tied with a chocolate box ribbon, she is the complete antithesis of the pale-faced, ethereal sylph 'with a smile hovering round her mouth like a butterfly round a flower'. It is the sylph in chrysalis stage whom we are watching, as she performs her complicated routine, first hanging on to the *barre*, wooden counterpart to the hands of a partner, next in the centre of the room where the

7

most poetic of *adagios* becomes at first merely a harass‑
ing problem.

The fact that the tyro will inevitably have hit upon
during the performance is the dancer on tiptoe (*sur
les pointes*), but to his disappointment this will not
occupy much time as he watches the class, at most
ten minutes in an hour for the elder pupils, perhaps
on that particular day not at all. To the teacher and
the dancer the 'point' is not the beginning and the
end of dancing, it is a part, and by no means the most
important, of a whole system. It is no isolated marvel,
not even a particularly difficult feat. Its development is
strictly logical physically whether it is used or not,
since every part of the body comes into play, and
under certain circumstances it is aesthetically neces‑
sary to suggest lightness, the take‑off for a flight or
even the flight itself, as in *The Swan*, those marvellous
pas de bourrées[1] that Pavlova knew how to perform so
superlatively. Also it is mechanically necessary in
certain gyratory movements.

To rise onto the points and move comes almost
natural to many, including men (E. G. Cossack
dancers without block shoes), and in any case it
never takes long to acquire. I must insist upon this

[1] See page 111.

8

just now and even deal with it proportionately at too great a length, because of the absurd misnomer of ballet as 'toe-dancing', and also, because it is invariably made the main grounds for ignorant attacks on ballet as being unnatural. Of course ballet is un-

natural, as unnatural as every form of the theatre, as unnatural as playing the piano, the fiddle, the drum or the triangle, but, if by unnatural they mean that it can only be acquired after much time and suffering, that is an absurdity. There are some whose feet are formed in such a way that the use of the points presents unusual difficulties, but the good teacher will immediately realise that and force nothing. It is only the indifferent teacher who turns ballet dancing into toe dancing and so deforms the feet and legs of her pupils. Alas, such teachers abound, for this is a difficult art to teach, and only a score or so in the world are capable of producing really fine dancers, and then the economic situation demanding undue haste turns against them. The first essential is to place the body of the pupil correctly; once that is done, and it takes time and vast knowledge, such pleasing things as points, turns, beats and jumps can soon be added. In Russia, where teaching had been developed into a fine art, the pupil learnt only at the *barre* for some two years before beginning to dance independently. In these days with a rapid living to be earned that is not possible, but fortunately the healthier bodies of the young girls of to-day mitigate somewhat the effects of this undue haste.

Dancing is essentially an aristocratic art, where pedigree plays a rôle of prime importance. The great dancer is taught by the great dancer so that within very few generations we can arrive at the very origins of the classical dance itself at the court of Louis XIV.

Nothing is written down, it is like a story told in

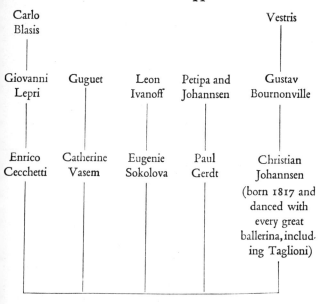

ANNA PAVLOVA

AND HER TEACHERS

An artistic pedigree that shows her to be only three generations
removed in a direct line from Vestris and Carlo Blasis

(I am much indebted to Monsieur Dandré for this information)

NOTE: The artistic pedigrees of Egorova, Kchesinska,
Preobrajenska, Trefilova are, of course, equally direct. Their
pupils, Baronova, Toumanova, Riabouchinska and the others
are therefore also in this line.

the bazaars of the Orient, handed down from generation to generation, gradually enriched as it passes through some original mind, modified by fashion yet in its essentials unchanged. Tradition does not prevent experiment or growth. The great dancer is the one who has absorbed the tradition, and who can add to it and leave it the richer at her death. The great dancer is creative and creators are rare: Camargo, Sallé, Heinel, Taglioni, Ellsler, Zucchi, Pavlova. We honour their memory. To the dancer they are immortal. Every time she *pirouettes*[1] she honours Heinel, who first developed it, when she amazes us by her dazzling *fouettés*,[1] she pays a tribute to Legnani, who carried her virtuosity to the stages and schools of Russia, soon to be spread throughout the world. Whether the small dancer of to-day knows these names or not they are a part of her, she dances differently because they danced. She too has a chance of becoming a part of the structure of ballet.

Let us follow the fortunes of one young pupil, happily unaware of what is expected of her in the future, unaware of the difficulties of dancing like Pavlova, the memory of whose perfections may

[1] See pages 93, 111.

12

have inspired her mother to take her to dancing school.

Mary is nine as she clutches the *barre* for the first time in the studio of a great *ballerina*. She starts well, for she has a finely proportioned body and a head that promises beauty. Without those attributes it would scarcely be worth starting at all, though miracles have been known to happen in the class-room, and bow legs to straighten themselves through the logical exercise,[1] also a squint can be corrected and even the most stubborn nose melt under the plastic surgeon's knife. The squint certainly matters, for *the body from hair to big toe is the dancer's instrument* and it must be as perfect as the virtuoso's fiddle or else all genius is a sorry waste. I rate beauty as an attribute exceedingly high.

A point that must be mentioned here under Beauty is the health of the dancer. More artists are ruined in looks and achievements through ill health than by any other cause, and a type of ill health that it is not always easy to detect. I have recently

---

[1] There is a recent case of a young boy with a diseased arm who was told that amputation was necessary—instead he joined a dancing class. To-day he is one of a company, if not a prominent artist at any rate a healthy athletic man.   A. L. H.

discussed this all important question at great length with a physician who has been the friend of all dancers from Pavlova to the smallest *coryphée*. The dancer is forced to eat at irregular hours and often, with the laudable object of keeping thin, prescribes for herself an unwise dietary backed up by various patent medicines. In practice nine times out of ten fatness in the dancer comes from no other reason than auto-intoxication, especially thick unshapely legs. This state of intoxication is so frequent and so little understood by the dancer or her parents that I must mention it here. The care of the liver and intestines may seem an unsavoury subject when discussing so poetical an art, but it is highly relevant to the sylphide in the chrysalis stage and should be thoroughly understood by every teacher. If an army marches on its stomach, the sylph dances on hers. A normal girl with the amount of exercise she takes as a dancer should require no strict or special diet to remain slim, while to be skinny, a living skeleton, is more unsightly by far than to be plump. Will Mary's mother kindly note.

For the first two years at least Mary will make various movements, most of them difficult, most of them apparently totally unrelated. Also, she will be so busy concentrating upon her feet that she will find it impossible to think of anything at all. As for being graceful, dismiss the idea. If she is a musical child, who once improvised her own dances, her parents will be bitterly disappointed at this sad falling-off, and will perhaps remove her to place her in some school where they teach gentle barefoot dances with scarf-wagging, flower-scattering and Pan-pipery. Then, if she has a bank account, in a few years' time she will be able to hire a theatre and for three ecstatic matinées to indulge in an orgy of self-expression, actually far less able to express herself than if she had remained in school a few years longer and acquired a perfect mastery of her body.

For the purposes of this study I have given Mary parents who are models of intelligence. They are doubtless a little mystified, but they have implicit trust in 'Madame', and so keep Mary at school, hoping for better things and happy at any rate that she has made more progress than Vera, who came at the same time. After these first years her feet will move without so great a mental effort. She will begin to appreciate the fact that these steps can be combined, that certain corresponding positions of the arms are helpful and, most important of all, that

15

the music is telling her things, those things that she used to hear before she went to dancing class.

Then a little time longer and Mary has a small dance arranged for her. In a pleasing, flattering, filmy white tarlatan she must face an audience com-

posed chiefly of mothers and aunts, a terrifying audience, for there could be nothing more viciously critical than a mother defending her young from the achievements of others. Perhaps she is frightened and does not give of her best, but she has gained experience. The very next time she remem-

bers what has been most effective, she can now
realise that she is pleasing her audience, that she can
make it applaud her; a thrilling emotion that immediately compensates her for the past sarcasms of
her teacher and her aching muscles. There is definite
contact, time to feel and to think, even while she is
turning, leaping or beating a series of *entrechats*.[1] From
a clumsy inexpressive leggy little girl she is becoming
a personality. Now, when she looks into the mirror,
if she escapes a swollen head (a large if), she can
criticise herself. The vast majority who begin dancing never attain this stage. She is an exception.
'*Dance with your head*', Pavlova told all pupils. Mary
is dancing with her head. She has now reached as
far as the gifted intelligent girl can go. Whether she
is to be a true artist or not depends upon many things
that are beyond her control, though, if she is really
clever, she can pass for one with many people besides
her own parents and their circle.

She is sixteen, ready to leave school and join a
company, but she will never have finished learning.
Pavlova took her lesson, stood the criticism of
another person to her dying day. From now on the
classes will be with the object of eradicating faults

[1] See page 111.

17

rather than of building up something new. The true lessons will be learnt on the stage and in the rehearsal room.

Mary has almost grown into one of those sylphs whom we have been watching.

III

THE CHOREOGRAPHER

SHE has passed under the control of a new person, the choreographer, who will use her, one amongst many, to fulfil a particular artistic function, to be a note in his complicated score. Her reactions to the problems he sets will determine her whole future.

This word choreographer is not as complicated as it sounds. It merely signifies the author of the movement, the arranger of the dances. But the function itself, as we shall see, is highly complicated, comprising the elements of sculpture, painting, music and the drama. Any competent dancer can arrange a small dance, especially for herself, by drawing upon various *enchainements* (combinations of steps) with which she is familiar. *It is the choreographer's function to orchestrate dancing,* the difference between picking out a melody on the piano with two fingers and presenting that melody scored for a large symphony orchestra.

19

IV

THE FUNCTIONS OF CHOREOGRAPHY

LIKE the sculptor the choreographer is concerned with the single figure and its relation to the group, like the carver his limitations lie in his particular medium; in the first case the block of stone, in the second the human body.

Like the painter he is concerned with background, foreground and space composition.

These comparisons are very real, but they can be carried no further, for up to now we have seen him merely as the designer of *tableaux vivants*, and it is a comparatively simple thing to create effective groups in human material. The particular problem that confronts the choreographer is getting the individuals into the groups and then in getting them out again. Ballet is not static, and it is in the transition from pose to pose, group to group, that the highest skill lies. Many a *maître de ballet* has gained credit and applause through a careful arrangement of his subjects in imitation of the figures on a Greek vase, a Roman sarcophagus or a Gothic cathedral. It is essential to realise that however effective this may be it does not constitute ballet. It is but the raw material from which ballets can be made. The choreographer must construct hundreds of pictures, hundreds of groups of statuary during the course of a single ballet, and it is out of his imagination that all the transition movements must come. Great knowledge without imagination is insufficient.

V

DRAMA AND BALLET

Next there is the very close relationship to drama. All theatre is a convention; a convention of time, space and the fourth wall. The particular convention of ballet is that the story is told in motion by silent actors, acted in pantomime without the aid of words. The drama therefore must be simple in situation and self-evident. *All programme descriptions are totally unnecessary for the understanding or enjoyment of good ballet.* According to this convention the choreographer can express in one direction much more than the dramatist and in another much less.

Take, for instance, the case of *Petrouchka*, the most moving drama in the whole of ballet, in some respects in the whole of the theatre. The programme story (not necessary for its understanding) runs as follows:

The scene is laid in Admiralty Square, St.

Petersburg, about 1830. In the midst of the
Carnival merry-making, there appears an old
magician of Oriental aspect, who displays to
the crowd his animated puppets, Petrouchka,
the Dancer, and the Moor, who perform a
brisk dance.

By his enchantments the magician has en-
dowed them with human attributes and senti-
ments. Petrouchka has the most humanity of
the three, and, therefore, suffers most from the
cruelty of the magician, who keeps him a
prisoner, aloof from human life. He feels deeply
his enslavement, his ugliness and his grotesque
appearance. He seeks consolation in the love of
the Dancer, and is on the point of believing his
suit successful, when she is frightened by his
uncouth manners.

The Moor is quite different. He is stupid and
spiteful, but richly attired, and the Dancer is
captivated by his sumptuous appearance. She
succeeds in fascinating him, but, at the moment
when they are ready to declare their love,
Petrouchka comes to interrupt them with a
jealous scene. Furious, the Moor throws him
out.

The carnival is at its height. A merchant who is out for a frolic, escorted by a couple of gypsy girls, throws banknotes among the crowd; coachmen and nursemaids join in a dance; a dancing bear is led through the crowd by his attendant, and finally masked revellers break into a mad dance.

Suddenly cries are heard from the magician's booth; the rivalry of Petrouchka and the Moor assumes a tragic turn. The puppets escape from the booth, the Moor pursuing Petrouchka, whom he fells to the ground with his scimitar. Petrouchka dies in the snow in the midst of the crowd, and a policeman fetches the magician who reassures the bystanders by proving to them that Petrouchka is only a puppet, with a wooden head and a body stuffed with sawdust. The crowd disperses, but, left alone, the magician to his consternation sees Petrouchka on the roof of his booth, threatening him and deriding the people who have been deceived.

Give the characters words to speak and it would take on a meaning more definite than even this programme synopsis, but it would narrow its scope, for as it stands at present it may fairly be taken to represent: the dawn of intelligence and the struggle for self-expression of the underdog, the *moujik* (Modern Russian interpretation), the triumph and final resurrection of the soul, the birth of the imagination stimulated by love; the composer himself sees in it the saga of 'the eternal and unhappy hero of all fairgrounds and all countries', the character in which Charlie Chaplin in *silent* film has gained the sympathy of the whole world. All these implications and many more have been read into *Petrouchka*, which, because of its very silence, becomes universal drama, the tragedy of everyman.

Ballet can tell of the tragedy of death in *The Swan*, of the exquisite story of the awakening of a young girl in *Le Spectre de la Rose*, a choreographic poem that would lose everything through being made more positive.

Fokine, the creator of these works, has proved himself a master in his understanding of the subtle relationship between drama and ballet, in taking full advantage of its wordlessness. Indeed, he stands almost alone in giving ballet its full scope dramatically, by not pinning it down too closely to literature. His *Thamar* and *Schéhérazade*, more definitely stories

with positive dramatic happenings, have not survived
as unimpaired by time, in spite of their magnificent
grouping and clear development of character, as

have *Carnaval*, *Petrouchka*, *Le Spectre de la Rose* and
that ballet of one person *The Swan*, which has only
died because no one has dared challenge comparison
with Pavlova.

It is in richness of emotional content, in the

liberty that its very vagueness allows to the imagina⁄
tion that the choreographer gains over the dramatist.
In complication of plot he is the loser, and, if forget⁄
ful of his medium, he oversteps the mark, then his
work is bad. That, at any rate, is one very definite
rule that can be stated on paper.

Within our convention it is possible to speak of
realism since in art all realism is relative. I will return
to this important point in its appropriate place.[1]

[1] Page 46 *et seq.*

VI

MUSIC AND BALLET

T HERE now remains the most important of all, the relationship of ballet to music.

There are many who would see dancing as an independent art, and who loudly clamour for the freedom of the dance from music. Serge Lifar, choreographer and *premier danseur* of the Paris Opera, oldest home of the dance, has recently published a manifesto urging this, and from an examination of his arguments we can most easily gauge the various possible relationships.

He says:

> Who is it who has placed our art in its present position? Who has made it the slave of a magnificent but despotic master? Music. All of us, both choreographers and dancers. And it is time to say that it is not music that has enslaved us, but we ourselves who have of our

own free will accepted the shackles whose weight is only now beginning to be felt. . . .

When one art wishes to illustrate another that art suffers a fatal loss of independence. The art of the dance, in former days the most beautiful, the freest and the most independent, has had to suffer in this way and has become the slave of music. *Duncanism*, a new word that first appears at the dawn of the twentieth century, was the force behind this bondage and has separated ballet and the dance more and more. Duncanism wished to illustrate a musical work independently of the rhythmic and dancing qualities that it might possess. The slogan of the twentieth century, 'there is no musical work that cannot be danced', whether it be a choral of Bach or a symphonic picture by Debussy, penetrated into the dance and became altered into 'there is no musical work that cannot be illustrated'.

Before we analyse these shrewd comments of the choreographer, who made his name with his ballet on Beethoven's *Prometheus*, it is necessary to look at the position of music in recent ballet history.

The nineteenth century was poor in its music for

ballet, for music was sharply divided into unqualified music and into an altogether inferior category, 'ballet music', something that had to be facile in emotion and obvious in rhythm. It could be ordered almost by the yard and cut about as so much material with no damage to the whole. The favourite composers were Minkus and Pugni, excellent craftsmen, to whom it would be agony to listen in the concert hall. Such composers of merit as Delibes and Tchaikovsky were exceptions, and the latter's first ballet *The Swan Lake* had a poor reception from the critics, who found it totally unsuited to ballet and fit only for the concert hall. Then Isadora Duncan dared dance to the classics, and in spite of some abuse her work found favour with the Russian *intelligentsia*; she had indicated a new direction, a rich field awaiting exploitation. Fokine had already worked out these questions for himself and required no prompting, but he was a member of an ultra-conservative institution, so that her courage and success inspired him and made the reception of his ideas so much easier. This led to a whole period of the adaptation of ballet to already existing music, what Lifar terms illustration. From this period comes *Carnaval* to Schumann, *Les Sylphides* to Chopin, *Le Spectre de la Rose* to Weber,

Thamar to Balakireff, *Cleopatra* to a whole group of composers, *Schéhérazade* to Rimsky-Korsakov. After these first ballets, with the discovery of Stravinsky, Diaghileff relied almost exclusively on commissioned works, interesting the leading and most advanced musicians of the day in the medium. It is only four years after his death that a return has been made to the use of pure music with Massine's symphonic ballets *Les Présages* (Tchaikovsky 5th symphony) and *Choreartium* (Brahms 4th symphony). This has been hailed as an innovation, but in fact it is merely a return to the principle upon which *Les Sylphides* was created, an innovation in extent alone.

Lifar objects not only to the *Sylphides* principle, but also to the use of commissioned music, with the argument that from the moment the dancer claims that all music is his province the composer says, 'You can dance everything? Well then, dance my composition', the possible result being that the composer, ignorant of ballet, unaware of the possibilities of the human body, writes variations of from six to seven minutes, when only two or three minutes are theatrically possible. This, as we shall see, is scarcely a feasible argument, but before discussing the subject as a whole let us see Lifar's solution. He suggests that writing down of movement, or its filming without music and only then commissioning music to suit the movement.

We have therefore to review three possible relationships between music and dancing: (i) making the ballet to existing music, (ii) making the ballet to specially commissioned music, (iii) making the music to an already arranged ballet.

(i) We start with the knowledge that this particular relationship has produced masterpieces, a whole series of works that bear repeated revival. Ballet is a theatrical art, it requires a theme to interpret, movement alone is not enough, and moreover movement alone will rapidly degenerate into the literary idea. Music supplies this theme. It not only inspires the choreographer, but the dancers. It is their continual link with him. The word 'illustration' describes inaccurately what actually occurs. It is possible to illustrate something positive like an episode in a book, impossible to illustrate anything as intangible as music. Music does not enslave the choreographer, it stimulates his imagination. The fact that it also imposes certain conditions does not imply slavery. The human body imposes its conditions, to escape from which one might equally well postulate the use of marionettes. Complete freedom is an impossible fallacy, only agreeable to coquette with on paper. All art implies slavery to its particular medium.

The chief objection to this particular relationship comes from the other side, from the musician, who invariably objects that the dancer is insensitive to music. He is often right, particularly in cases where piano music has been adapted to orchestra, but again, even here, he is more right on paper than in fact. It is impossible to view such a complex struc⁄ture as ballet from any one specialised angle, either musical or choreographic. It is here a question of the theatre and not the concert hall and it is the general theatrical effect that counts. *Carnaval*, *Les Sylphides* and *Le Spectre de la Rose*, orchestrated originally by the best musicians of the day, are so closely related in form and feeling to the music that it would be absurd to accuse Fokine of a lack of musical taste. Music has been *applied* to the theatre.

(ii) Again we start with the knowledge that this particular relationship has produced masterpieces: *Petrouchka* (Stravinsky−Fokine), *Le Tricorne* (da Falla−Massine), *L'Oiseau de Feu* (Stravinsky−

Fokine), to isolate but three of such works that have endured.

The only objection that is urged against this is the fact that the music may be unsuitable. If that is the case, then someone has blundered and badly so. The method is not to blame. In actual practice with *The Sleeping Princess*, Petipa worked in the closest harmony with Tchaikovsky, showing him clearly what was needed for the dance, *L'Oiseau de Feu* was another such close collaboration between Fokine and Stravinsky. It must never become a case of ordering the music and then hoping for the best.

In this case even less than in the first can one talk of slavery and illustration. Who is the slave, the composer who is confined to a certain timing and style or the choreographer who must make movements based on the music?

Actually this method of collaboration is the ideal, the logical relationship between music and the dance, though it calls for the intervention of an unknown quantity, X, that I have yet to discuss.

(iii) This third suggested relationship is untried, not that that is in itself against it.

There are certain immediate objections. From

where is the choreographer's initial idea to come?
Must all ballet be entirely abstract? This would be
theatrically ineffective. *Choreartium* is wrongly called
an abstract ballet, it is without a connected theme,
but it is directly inspired by Brahms. It is not just
so much movement for its own sake. The very
nature of the human medium makes dancing for
the sake of pattern alone an impossibility. A dancer
is much more than a moving portion of a design.
She will force a meaning of her own into anything
abstract. Moreover, according to this notion, actually
the slavery of the composer, there are two certain
dangers, the one I have mentioned, of writing a
story, illustrating it (yes, really illustrating this time)
and then fitting the music to it, or of turning the
dance into acrobacy. This is the method of the
acrobat turned cabaret dancer. 'I will use my own
movements that proved such a success at Olympia
Circus last Christmas and the conductor will im-
provise some sort of music'.

There is a fallacy of which much is made that the
dance existed primitively without music. It was invariably accompanied by percussion or chanting of
some kind. The most primitive peoples do not dance
in silence. Is it possible or in any way desirable for us

to return to the tom-tom? That is what the complete subservience of music implies.

Lifar, in publishing his manifesto, has greatly aided the cause of ballet by forcing people to analyse it, and by crying out against certain abuses that are very current to-day. The general popularisation of the symphonic ballet, for instance, would be a disaster, both musical and choreographic. Only a master can dare tackle it, and then but rarely. Lifar is right when he denies the dangerous and misleading slogan, 'there is no musical work that cannot be danced'. There is a whole field of music that could not be danced *effectively* from a theatrical viewpoint; only theoretically is the slogan true.

That his own suggestion is not generally valid he will soon discover in practice, though it may produce a work or two of beauty.

The one certain rule in Ballet creation is that there can be no rule save a knowledge and respect for the medium.

VII

NOVERRE ON THE CHOREOGRAPHER

BOTH Noverre, great *maître de ballet* of the eighteenth century, and later Fokine, have laid down in a series of dicta drawn from their experience certain guiding principles for the choreographer.

The ideal choreographer, says Noverre, must be an absolute autocrat.[1] He must know everything and attend to every detail himself. He must be well grounded in painting, since 'his art has in view the same object as the painter's'. He must be well acquainted technically with music, for 'the choice of good music is as essential to the dance as the choice of words to the orator . . . also, he will furnish the composer with the principal points of his action'. In this he anticipates Lifar's objections. Noverre also insists upon some scientific knowledge, anatomy to

[1] Noverre certainly was. He would spit at his dancers in his rage.

rectify errors in the dancers, and 'a smattering of
geometry will also be found of great advantage'. But
all this does not yet satisfy him. Since he defines
ballet as 'Nature embellished with all the charms of
art', the choreographer must study Nature at close
quarters. He must, for instance, study the jealous
man 'to observe the shades and differences of expression upon his face' so that he will be able to add to
ballet a dramatic element, for, 'if the grand passions
are suited to tragedy, they are no less necessary to
pantomime'. He postulates not only a knowledge of
literature, 'the success of ballet depends for a large
part upon a choice of subject', but also for that fine
discrimination that can avoid pitfalls by a continual
awareness of the nature of the medium, 'there are a
quantity of things that cannot be rendered intelligible
by gesture'.

Noverre's advice, given over 175 years ago, remains sound to the present day. For a long time,
however, it was completely ignored. Dancing was
indulged in, to use his own words, 'for the sake of
dancing, as if all consists in the action of the legs
alone'. When that happened it became impossible
to distinguish between acrobacy and dancing since
the dividing line is always narrow. Fortunately

on occasions an individual artist could succeed in spite of choreographic handicaps in moving one, a fact that saved ballet, but it was quite exceptional.

VIII

PRE-FOKINE SURVIVALS

Giselle, created in 1841, the oldest ballet in the current repertoire, is a case in point. The music by Adolphe Adam is banal in the extreme, the choreography complex technically but not emotionally and the story deeply romantic, an absolute contradiction of both music and choreography. Clearly a ballet that would have earned the disapproval of Noverre. It is because of the story and the genius of a few *ballerinas* that this work has survived.

It tells of a care-free, happy village maiden, cruelly betrayed, who loses her reason and commits suicide. She becomes a *willi*, a species of vampire, who tempts men to their doom in the woodland graveyard at night. A conventional enough story in the true romantic pattern of Udolpho, but the dramatic scope it gives to the dancer is enormous. In the first act she is a laughing, healthy girl, then comes the crisis, the scene of insanity when no longer able to control her limbs, mechanically she tries to recapture the movements of her dance, then violence and suicide. In the next act there is complete calm. She is no longer human, a disembodied spirit, gliding over the tombstones.

In this ballet Anna Pavlova, in spite of the handicaps I have mentioned, succeeded in rising to such heights of acting that she could make her audience first shudder, then cry. With her death *Giselle* has sunk into a long sleep, to survive only as a period curiosity until such time as another genius arrives to make it live again.

The other pre-Fokine works that survive,[1] and with every right, are those which Marius Petipa created in partnership with Tchaikovsky, *The Swan Lake* and *The Sleeping Princess*. To a large extent they obey the dicta of Noverre and while they are basically dancing for the sake of dancing they possess a dramatic content that the dancer cannot ignore.

The Swan Lake is an involved and dramatic story expressed in dancing and conventional mime. To us

---

[1] Tchaikovsky's *Casse-Noisette* and Delibes' *Coppelia* are still in the repertoire. It takes a genius to make these museum pieces tolerable in spite of the charm of their music.

to-day much of it may seem old-fashioned, it contains long digressions that hold up the action, but Marius Petipa was a true pioneer, the father of modern ballet. Diaghileff's one act version has given *The Swan Lake* a new life in which the dancer has every opportunity to reveal technique, individuality and dramatic power. To-day Petipa's works remain the finest training ground both for dancer and audience.

IX

THE ADVENT OF FOKINE

IT is Petipa's pupil, Michael Fokine, however, who truly rediscovered Noverre's dicta and restated them both in word and in practice. *It is important to note that Fokine did not proceed by revolution but by evolution.* There has been no ballet revolution, the tradition has remained intact.

One of Fokine's first most original and daring creations was *The Swan*, made so famous by Pavlova that it is easy to neglect its importance as a ballet. I see it as a complete manifesto of the new, the contemporary school.[1] This will be more evident when we compare it to previous bird dances, always a favourite theme in classical ballet. Petipa's birds reveal firstly their

[1] I am not suggesting that *The Swan* was a *conscious* manifesto on Fokine's part, merely a reflection of his state of mind at the time. He selected the Saint-Saëns music, which had deeply moved him, and the dance itself was set for Anna Pavlova in an hour or so. She was definitely a collaborator in this work in the sense that her particular genius inspired him. It must remain hers for ever.— A. L. H.

lightness, they leap and flutter to the accompaniment of brilliant music. They are essentially an opportunity for the *ballerina* to show her virtuosity. The Blue Bird (*Aurora's Wedding*) remains the most pure and beautiful of all virtuoso numbers. Fokine's bird, on the contrary, is the actor in a drama of life and death, of struggle, in which the inspiration as well as the accompaniment comes from the music. With Petipa immobility is negative, it means the end of the dance; with Fokine it is positive, it means Death. Petipa's bird must smile in the manner of the well-trained dancer, incidentally a difficult thing to do; Fokine's Swan must interpret the tragedy implicit in the music. The first is a brilliant dance, the second both dance and drama combined, hence I call it a ballet. So it is in all Fokine's works, even in what is technically a *suite de danses* such as *Les Sylphides*, where the word 'drama' is too strong and the word 'dance' alone inadequate to describe what is occurring. Fokine in his use of the dramatic element is invoking not literature but music.

Before his day there was a complex story, more or less ignored. The relationship between dance, music and drama was haphazard. It is Fokine who rediscovered the ideal balance and revived ballet as an art.

X

FOKINE'S FIVE POINTS

IN 1910, in a letter to *The Times*, Fokine laid down the principles upon which he was work-ing. Taken together with Noverre's letters they state the last word upon the subject of choreography. These are his points:

(i) To invent in each case a new form of movement, corresponding to the subject and character of the music, instead of merely giving combinations of ready-made steps.

Previously the scene of a ballet might be laid in Spain (*Don Quixote*), in India (*Brahma*) or in the Venusberg (*Tannhäuser*), but the type of dancing would be identical, always on the points with the *grand pas de deux* always in the same place and the inevitable smile that all too frequently degenerated into a toothy grin. So little heed was paid to style that it was customary for the *ballerina* to insert in the middle her own most popular dance with no damage to the whole, an obvious impossibility in a Fokine ballet; imagine a Russian dance in *Carnaval* or *Les Sylphides* for instance!

> (ii) Dancing and gesture in ballet have no meaning unless they serve as an expression of dramatic action.

This is the common-sense law of every storyteller that each phrase and each character must advance the story towards its climax, and that nothing extraneous can be allowed to remain.

> (iii) To admit the use of conventional gesture only when it is required by the style of the ballet, and in all other cases to replace the gestures of the hands by movements of the whole body. *Man can and should be expressive from head to foot.*

This means the end of hand placed on heart equals love, and similar formulae that can be imported into any work and that have become so mechanical that they no longer have any meaning. In practice, on that very account, they are extremely difficult to perform without provoking laughter. It is indeed a test of the highly trained *premier danseur classique* to see him perform the mimed portions of *The Swan Lake* with dignity, grace and conviction.

Acting is now a part of dancing; the expression of the face, the head, shoulders and back as much an indication of the mood as the hands. *Le Spectre de la Rose* is a duet of love, yet not once does the rose place his hands to his heart or his lips. The angle of his body and head as he leans over the chair, the gestures of his arms, all too often made into a meaningless and frenzied milling motion, all show the tenderness that she dreams he is feeling. In *Carnaval* where Harlequin removes his heart and lays it broken at Columbine's feet the definitely artificial style of the period demands so conventional a gesture, Fokine's only exception.

Like Noverre, Fokine is a close student of Nature, analysing every type of movement and translating it into terms of ballet. There is no greater indication of character than gesture. The earliest signs of insanity can be observed in the manner of a handshake. By this dictum Fokine brings ballet into closer contact with Nature and postulates a definite ballet realism.

Realism in ballet means a rigid adherence to style and consistency of treatment within a work. Once the ballet convention has been accepted then every-

thing that follows must be plausible, and have a truth of its own. Grinning dancers on their points in the Venusberg grot are unrealistic, but that the rose should dance as it does with the dreaming maiden, that Papillon should move swiftly on her points, the Swan float across the stage in a *pas de bourrée* is entirely realistic. *Schéhérazade, Igor, Thamar* or *Narcisse* on the points would be a crime against true style. When in *Eunice* Fokine produced the first ballet off the points there was an outcry. 'Our school has worked for generations to put our dancers on their points and now he wants to take them off again', said the enraged Russian *balletomanes*, and the victory for realism was won in Western Europe before it found its way back to Russia.

There are exceptions where a Greek ballet is danced on the points, *Mercury* (Massine–Satie) or *Apollon Musagètes* (Balanchine–Stravinsky), but in those cases there is a very definite stylisation, a deliberate artificiality and no mixture of styles. Fokine himself, however, has never used nor admitted the use of such stylisation.

Also with this dictum of Fokine's the whole vocabulary of ballet is enlarged. The many dances of peasant and popular origin can be incorporated into ballet, without undue stylisation, and what is called character dancing comes triumphantly into its own with such masterpieces as the Polovtsian dances from *Prince Igor* (Fokine–Borodin) and *The Three Cornered Hat* (Massine–da Falla), ushering in a new field of music, of décor and costume.

When the opponents of the ballet system rail against its dated artificiality they are clearly thinking of the days before 1905 and the emergence of Fokine, days that still exist in many opera-houses the world over.

> (iv) The group is not merely an ornament. The new ballet advances from the expressive-ness of the face or the hands to that of the whole body, and from that of the individual body to groups of bodies and the expressiveness of the combined dancing of a crowd.

This again is a plea for the *rapprochement* of music and action, for a more complex orchestration of motion, for a choreographic counterpoint. Also it completely alters the status of the dancer. Instead of one brilliant individual and a mechanical group in the back-ground there must now be an *ensemble* of dance artists, whose function it is to interpret instead of merely being occupied in keeping time and keeping line. One grinning mechanical *coryphée* will immediately upset the whole balance. Gone for ever are the days when an individual of genius can save a whole work. Diaghileff said of *Les Sylphides*, 'There is no *corps de ballet*, but an ensemble of sensitive artists'.

(v) The alliance of dancing on equal terms with the other arts. The new ballet does not demand 'ballet music' from the composer, nor 'tutus' and pink satin slippers from the designer; it gives complete liberty to their creative powers.

XI

DECOR AND COSTUME

WE have already dealt with the subject of music. Décor and costume have undergone a very similar evolution from the professional 'stage artist', who built his grandiose and clumsy sets according to a naturalism that ill accorded with the convention of ballet, to the easel artist who saw in the theatre a medium that appealed to him much as the fresco appealed to the artists of the Italian Re-naissance. It is in the theatre that the Russian artist, for so many generations a copyist of Western Europe, France or Germany, found himself and formed a school that has influenced and taught the entire world.

This school was composed of men such as Benois, Bakst, Korovin, Golovin, Doboujinsky, Roerich and others, who were admirably suited by their training and outlook for a work that meant compromise with and a knowledge of the sister arts. Grouped round Diaghileff and Benois, the most erudite and cultured of all artists and the finest practical theatrical mind of the age, they were familiar with the history of past civilisations, with music and the drama. They could conceive of the finished work as a picture, harmonious in its every detail. So meticulous were they in the matching of colour that they would search the markets for pieces of old brocade that would enhance the general effect. No makeshift or approximation could meet with their approval, yet for all this care they possessed an originality and a sense of colour that was revolutionary. It is as a colourist, daring in the extreme, that Bakst first startled the world (and himself by his success), yet in 1935 when *Thamar* and *Schéhérazade* were revived with their colours sadly faded, one could appreciate the magnificence of the drawing, the noble perspectives, the composition that astonished both by its nobility and its science. This first, the pre-war period of décor has never been equalled. It was brought about by artists who lived in the theatre and for the theatre.

A number of circumstances made a change of school necessary. Encouraged by Larionov and Gontcharova, painters of fine talent, Diaghileff explored the grotesque and found his way into the studios of Paris. With Picasso (*Three Cornered Hat, Parade, Pulcinella*) and Derain (*La Boutique Fantasque*) ballet found inspired work, but now the artist needed constant inspiration or his work was a failure. It was a case of hit or miss. After the first galaxy of talent there was never the same feeling for the stage. All too often the successful painter used ballet for *réclame* instead of forming a part of it.

Since the original Russian group there has been no school with definite characteristics. The parallel with modern furniture is a very close one. There are many remarkable pieces, but no strong guiding principle. This has been more than ever the case since the death of Diaghileff. The guiding principle with the Russian decorative school was a unity of purpose with the choreographer. Benois devised stories and indicated their treatment, Bakst conceived the form and movement of *L'Après-midi d'un Faune*. To-day one can safely say that décor is the least important of all the elements. It is an embellishment and not a necessity and costume, one of the biggest factors in moulding the dance, has now been divorced from it. The two most important productions of our day, *Les Présages* and *Choreartium*, actually gain when seen in the black and white of practice dress. *Jeux d'Enfants* (costumes Mirò), *Cotillon* (Berard) and *Concurrence* (Derain) alone gain in costume and are given added meaning. It is no mere coincidence that they are planned by Boris Kochno, for so many years Diaghileff's lieutenant.

When the painter works in close harmony with the choreographer as did Benois and Bakst, the blending of colour becomes an integral part of the choreography. For that reason the redressing of *Carnaval*, sometimes attempted, is nothing short of vandalism. 'It shows Fokine in a new light', say its defenders, not realising that for a different style of costume and a different scale of colours Fokine would have produced different movement.

Yet in the majority of cases to-day décor and costumes are commissioned and only arrive at the very last moment when the ballet has been finally set. In such a case success is purely a matter of luck. It should be a matter of plan.

XII

X, THE UNKNOWN QUANTITY

I⸺T will be seen from Fokine's conception of ballet what a delicate structure it had now become, a structure that required from the first germ of an idea the most precise and tactful balance between the arts.

Who could be the final arbiter when choreo grapher, composer and artist each held a brief for his own speciality? It is this function of arbiter that Diaghileff was the first to fulfil. In his life he accom plished many other things; without him it is certain that ballet could never have attained its present position as an art or have attracted to it the outstand ing artists of the day, but what is important for the purposes of this study is not his actual achievement as a man, but the particular function that he fulfilled, a function made essential from the moment that he, Fokine and Benois conceived the new ballet.

Diaghileff became the central clearing house for

ideas, some he rejected, others he directly inspired. He wedded certain music to certain paintings and then gently, almost imperceptibly, influenced the choreographer. He taught and moulded all those who came into contact with him.

Because throughout his quarter-century of active ballet work it is impossible to find his name in a programme as responsible for any one thing, many people have tried to reduce his rôle to the comparatively minor one of a great impresario. Nothing could be more untrue. Diaghileff was the unknown quantity, *X,* that became essential the instant that 'the alliance of dancing on equal terms with the other arts' was a ruling principle, and rapidly this mysterious *X* becomes of more and more importance. Companies of talented artists are sterile and collapse without it. It is the rarity of *X* and not of dancers, painters and musicians that has caused the huge gaps between Noverre and Fokine. To-day every ballet company relies for its success on the work of Serge Diaghileff in a proportion that is well over fifty per cent. The keynote of his productions was consistency. If they failed, then they failed as a whole, no element could be praised at the expense of the others.

The formula now reads X + choreographer + composer + painter + dancers = The Ballet.

I have called the vitalising figure, X, the unknown quantity, for a very definite reason, and not only to avoid confusion when discussing general principles, by using the name of an actual individual, Diaghileff. Our X is an unknown quantity, for there can be no definite rule as to how a ballet should originate. Under certain circumstances, if liaison is maintained throughout, absolutely no method is definitely wrong.

It can originate from a vague conception of movement, as when Jean Cocteau saw Anton Dolin indulging in acrobatics in a theatre corridor and immediately conceived of a sporting ballet. It can originate through the inspiration of a vague idea made more concrete by discussion, as when the words 'Pagan Russia' in the minds of Stravinsky, Roerich and Nijinsky grew into so ambitious a work as *Le Sacre du Printemps*, or through an artist's travels, as when Bakst returned from Greece, his head full of the bas-reliefs that became *L'Après-midi d'un Faune*. It can originate through the discovery of music as in *La Boutique Fantasque*, where the final result we know so well was arrived at after having first taken the form of an animated pack of cards (the Kings and Queens still survive) and then of a country fair. Constant discussion shapes and polishes the original notion, constant discussion *guided by X.*

Lately, in England in particular, many ballets have originated in still another manner, through paintings; *Job* (de Valois from Blake), *The Rake's Progress* (de Valois from Hogarth), *Gods Go a begging* (de Valois from Watteau), *Bar au Folies Bergères* (de Valois from Manet), *Foyer de la danse* (Ashton from Degas).

Inspiration from painting has been known by every choreographer, an obvious source of rich material. 'The history of ballet', says Massine, 'is but two hundred years old, the history of plastic art ageless.' In much of his own work he has drawn from Callot, Hogarth and Longhi. The method now so current in England of taking inspiration from the works of one painter is legitimate, but dangerous. The result is all too often static, a series of actual poses with either no dancing or the dancing out of character. In *Job* Ninette de Valois has made a conspicuous success.

Direct inspiration from music we have already discussed.

In practice these sources of inspiration are so

mixed, so much the result of a group of people interchanging ideas that it is rare to be able to analyse ballet creation with any certainty. Already with *Schéhérazade* it is a moot point who contributed the final idea. The score was played over, with Diaghileff, Bakst, Benois and Fokine each making some suggestion.

The result is the happiest where as in this case there is no too definite history.

XIII

THE SCENARIO

THE one approach that is surely wrong is the purely literary. Every choreographer, everyone connected with ballet, is inundated under a flow of long and complex scenarios, brilliant ideas for ballets. My own mail has from three to five a week the whole year round. These are invariably useless. No such extraneous idea can be of any value. Only one of the family, used to the atmosphere and technique of ballet, can fulfil this function.

The early days of ballet delve into mythology, Noverre is full of such material. Then the story passes through the romantic Hoffmanesque legend (*Giselle* and the like) into the gentler fairy-tale (*Sleeping Princess*, *Aladdin*). With the advent of Diaghileff, Fokine and the one-act ballet the story becomes either much slighter (*Carnaval*, *Spectre de la Rose*), or more condensed and dramatic (*Thamar*, *Schéhérazade*), definitely a development of character. Later it leaves the romantic far behind, treating of bouffe subjects in the Italian manner (*Good Humoured Ladies*, *Pulcinella*, *Scuola di Ballo*), and for a very short period giving a satirical commentary on life (*Les Biches*, *Le Train Bleu*, *Le Pas d'Acier*, *Pastorale Barabau*) or returning to pastoral classicism with a flippant modern slant (*Mercury*, *Apollon Musagètes*). These last two categories, however well and consistently done, inevitably show their age.

Once again the only rule is to study the nature of the medium. The story itself, if suitable, is relatively unimportant, it is the treatment that counts. Two of the most successful of modern ballets are *Cotillon* and *Concurrence*. Here are the programme stories; taken in connection with the ballets themselves they are highly instructive:

Cotillon.—The scene is laid in a ballroom where the following episodes take place.

The Introductions—The Master of Ceremonies turns up late and in a hurry. The Master and Mistress of Ceremonies demonstrate the first dance, which is repeated by the guests. A new *entrée* and dance of the hats— Harlequins, Jockeys and Spaniards. The Hand of Fate.—The cavalier comes up to the curtain to choose one of the hands that are revealed above it, but is stopped by the sudden apparition of a hand gloved in black. The Magic Lantern.—A young girl reads the fortune of the guests. Apparition of 'The Bat' and the 'Cup of Champagne'—Grand rondo and conclusion of the Cotillon.

Concurrence.—Everything passes into insignificance before the charm of fine raiment. Under its spell jealousies are aroused, passions inflamed, and even friendships destroyed.

Once upon a time there lived two tailors who vied with each other over the lavish display of beautiful clothes which each offered for sale. Their rivalry grew into a quarrel which became more bitter as the crowd, confused by the splendour and variety of the goods, vacillated, between the rival sellers.

Eventually the commotion and noise became so great that the inhabitants, jealous for the reputation of their well-ordered town, dispersed the animated crowd.

The tailors found themselves alone, but, well pleased with their profits, became reconciled.

These stories are nothing to read, barely under⁄ standable, and actually it is impossible to describe what is taking place on the stage. Indeed, in the second description the most important character of all, a young girl, is entirely omitted. Yet in action they are logical and satisfying; a vivid proof of the fact that treatment rather than story is important, and also of the necessity for the ingredient X. Both were written by Boris Kochno who as Diaghileff's lieutenant has had a close practical contact with ballet. They were jotted down on the back of an envelope.

A recent example of a fine balletic story is Constant Lambert's *Apparitions*. Conceived by a musician, it is a part of the music, and logical when it is taken in connection with that music.

These facts will, I hope, finally discourage the many who send their scenarios to the author for approval.

CHOREOGRAPHY SINCE FOKINE

HAD this been a history of choreography it would have been necessary for me to deal at considerable length with the post-Fokine choreographers, but what concerns us here is not the work of individuals however great, but the nature of ballet itself.

The change from Petipa to Fokine was a tremendous one, affecting basic principles, while there has been absolutely no constructive change after Fokine; ballet has merely expressed other things; romance has given place to satire. Moods alone have altered, form never. Indeed it is difficult to see how it could change since its main characteristic is a lack of rigidity and formalism that makes it the perfect vehicle for any theme, from cubistic propaganda (*Parade*) to Americana (*Union Pacific*), pure poetry (*Cotillon*) or symphonic composition (*Choreartium*).

A few notes, therefore, on the general tendencies

and outlook of Fokine's successors will suffice. This scant dismissal is no reflection on their ability as artists, merely a necessity demanded by the object of this study. The attributes required by the choreographer do not make it astonishing that he is scarcer than the artist in any other medium. In this whole study, covering a considerable and a singularly rich period, we are only concerned with some half-dozen names.

Nijinsky, Fokine's immediate successor and a dancer of genius, is sometimes credited with having revolutionised ballet. As we have seen, this cannot have been the case. There has never been a revolution, but an evolution, and that evolution was Fokine's. What Nijinsky actually accomplished, to introduce fresh hitherto non-balletic movements into ballet and thus to extend its scope, is all a part of the Fokine plan.

To-day, of all Nijinsky's work only *L'Après-midi d'un Faune* survives. One cannot ascribe to that any great influence in movement, for ballet *en profile* can only be used in a particular case that aims at a bas-relief effect. *Le Sacre du Printemps*, now passed out of the repertoire, and in Nijinsky's version never more than a *succès de scandale*, must have had a greater

influence since so large a company of dancers par-
ticipated in it, an indirect influence that made them
realise how with their training there existed types of
movement hitherto unexplored. This ballet must
have been a tonic and a stimulus that led the dancer
to lay aside not only a narrow conception of beauty
and grace but also all set notions of the type of
rhythm that could lend itself to choreography.
Through the dancer it eventually influenced the
public. In that respect and that respect only, whether
success or failure, it may be counted a pioneer work.
If we follow the general tendency and ascribe to it
anything more, our whole idea will be thrown out
of focus. The possibility of such a work was foreseen
vaguely by Noverre and very definitely by Fokine.

The most fertile development of movement is due
to Massine who has dominated ballet from his first
work, *Le Soleil de Nuit,* in 1915 till the present day.
He has developed character dancing and blended
it with pure classicism to a degree never before
attempted. The richness of his source material and
its stage translation in such works as *Les Présages* and
Choreartium is amazing. He has digested the museums
of the world, the popular dancing of all nations and
the recent developments in Central Europe till his

repertoire of movement is the most extensive in the history of ballet. His very faults come from over-richness, a tendency to exaggerate movement, yet like all great choreographers, and this is a test of artistry, both in dancer and choreographer, his very lack of movement is eloquent and is used with immense effect.

Bronislava Nijinska, great sister of the great Nijinsky, has produced works of first-class import-ance. Coming to choreography late and through teaching her forte lies not only in her exceedingly sensitive musical reactions but also in her use and development of the individual dancer, whose personality she knows how to exploit to an extra-ordinary degree. A Nijinska *corps de ballet* arrange-ment is very much a composition of combined soloists, blend of discipline and individuality. She has the ability of lending an intimate quality to the spectacular, of making virtuosity emo-tional. She actually succeeded in producing deeply moving work during the final Diaghileff phase when flippancy was the order of the day; even in such a frolic as *Les Biches* (English: *The House Party*) she explored beneath the surface, while *Les Noces* remains one of the most poignant of all ballet

memories, perhaps the last Diaghileff masterpiece. Nijinska understands not merely the dancer's technical possibilities, but her capacity for depth and emotion, even where the dramatic situation does not obviously call for emotion. In that respect she has greatly enriched not only ballet, but every dancer fortunate enough to come into contact with her. Nijinska has genius, the word is not too strong. So far insufficient use has been made of it, and for obvious reasons her magnificent work for Ida Rubinstein did not receive wide enough recognition. I have yet to meet anyone who can analyse ballet more clearly and more objectively. Well does she deserve Diaghileff's praise, "if I had a daughter I could wish one like Nijinska".

Georges Balanchine came at a time when ballet was at its lowest ebb, the final period of a Diaghileff wearied in his search for musical and decorative novelty. Deeply musical, even subtly musical, brilliant but not always in a sustained manner, his works do not always do him justice. Too often they are effective for one season and dead the next. Yet in a sense he has rediscovered the use of classical movement and by a very personal distortion given it a new significance. By outlook he is more directly an heir of Petipa than is Massine, more deeply in love with the past.

To him lies the credit of having launched the new ballet on its spectacular career. A great believer in the young and untried artists, it is for them that he has made his greatest works, *Cotillon* and *Concurrence*. Here he is brilliant throughout, and no one could show a more plastic outlook, one further removed from literature and nearer to music. The young girl in *Concurrence*, of no importance on paper, dominates the ballet, floats in and out linking together the diverse parts into a harmonious whole. This is the musician's approach and Balanchine is essentially a musician in approach, at times in fact too consciously, so over-subtle that in such a work as *Mozartiana* the result seems anti-musical.

He can produce a great work at intervals, but rarely a work that is just a competent piece of craftsmanship, a sound school piece. He is rapidly bored, a man who must create at fever heat. It is certain that his great work for Ballet is only just commencing. With his own company and in charge of the Metropolitan Opera ballet, in a new country with plenty of stimulus, he should become a major influence in the history of our art.

71

XV

ENGLISH CHOREOGRAPHY

THESE are the great names in modern ballet, the creators who have been able to enrich the dance within the framework discovered by Fokine.

Outside Russian ballet few choreographers have arisen. In England[1] we have been fortunate in producing Ninette de Valois and Frederick Ashton, who have advanced with rapidity from a fumbling apprenticeship to full mastery with the individuality that that implies. Ashton by his brilliance and Ninette de Valois by her depth and artistic integrity, with that splendid instrument that she has forged, 'The Vic-Wells ballet', hold the future of English ballet in their hands. Their opportunities are many. Each nation has its natural tempo and its characteristic

[1] Antony Tudor, like Frederick Ashton, a pupil of Marie Rambert at The Ballet Club, remarkable nursery for dancing, choreography and décor, shows very considerable promise for the future.

movements, product of physique and environment. It is for them now to found a truly national school, which, based on the Russian, should one day find supremacy as did the Russian based on the French and Italian combined.

Apart from a senseless chauvinism, nationality cannot be ignored in any study of an artistic move-ment. To-day both England and America are making rapid strides out of the apprentice stage. It is too early to attempt an analysis of their special charac-teristics. *Job* is an English ballet, even apart from the nationality of Blake and Vaughan Williams; *The Rake's Progress* is an unmistakably English product. In both, dancing without being neglected is made subservient to a study of character; that may be a possible clue, though it is not confirmed by Ashton's ballets or de Valois' other work. Plastic work that can be discussed in terms of literature is certainly favoured by a large section of our public.

A discussion of English choreography is out of place in a book relating to general principles, but what is strictly relevant and of prime importance is the condition of work at Sadler's Wells.[1] *It more*

[1] I write of Sadler's Wells as an impersonal body. Its success could not have come about without Miss Baylis's faith, courage

73

nearly reaches the ideal than is the case with any other ballet company to-day, and only a lack of important funds separates it from the attainment of that ideal.[1] The dancers there appear in public only twice a week, an essential for the maintenance of really first-class work, and a school is attached to the theatre.

With the skeleton of such a first-class system it will be a crime if lack of funds prevents its further development. Since no commercial aims are the incentive, the dancers are treated with the care that sensitive artists deserve. The work accomplished has been striking. It is now possible to say that our national company can hold its own with any without the need of hiding artistic deficiencies by a talk of patriotism. Given the necessary encouragement, and at once, this may well open a new chapter in the

and idealism, or Ninette de Valois' skill, knowledge and artistic integrity. There are others who have contributed to a brilliant whole, chief among them Marie Rambert at The Ballet Club, teacher and inspirer, who has provided so much material for successful exploitation by the larger company. I am not concerned with names here, but with a fact.—A. L. H.

[1] Should this catch the eye of some Maecenas will he drop me a line! No artistic investment would give a quicker or richer return. He (or She) would serve not only dancing, for, as we see, Ballet is the most comprehensive of the arts.—A. L. H.

history of ballet, and assume a world instead of a
national importance. Already Margot Fonteyn's
Swan Lake is memorable. It is many years since I
have seen her equal in this rôle, and she is adding
to it with each performance.[1] A system that can
allow of such development is clearly a very living
one. As till recently I have not greatly believed in
English effort and have proved myself in that respect
a poor prophet, these lines can not be read as an
outburst of chauvinism. I realise the distance still to
be travelled, but I know that the Vic-Wells ballet
is now in a sufficiently receptive state to begin the
journey.

[1] Her *Sylphides* also is outstanding. Perhaps some day Fonteyn
will bring *Giselle* back to life again (see page 41). There
are many signs to suggest this possibility; a quite unusual
combination of technique, artistry and charm.

XVI

CHOREOGRAPHY OUTSIDE THE CLASSICAL TRADITION

CLASSICAL ballet dancing is not the whole of dancing. That is an obvious truism. From the Fiji Islander to the Basque peasant, from the Granada gypsy to the Morris dancer in an English village, from the ceremonial of the Roman Church to the troupe of Tiller girls, all perform some type of dance without paying tribute to Carlo Blasis[1] or the Five positions.[2]

Ballet dancing is a scientific development of popular dancing, just as classical music is a scientific development of the folk song. Anyone who has seen those splendid Festivals organised by the English Folk Dance Society will realise that fact. There can be no antagonism between Folk dancing and Ballet, since the one is the theatrical development of the other. Folk dancing is indulged in for the

[1] See page 101.　　　　[2] See page 108.

pleasure of the performer, while in ballet the aim is the pleasure of the observer. That point must be clearly understood.

It is not my present object to deal with dancing outside of ballet, except in so far as doing so serves the better to explain ballet.

There have been many 'new' schools of dancing, arising from Isadora Duncan, an individual genius, from Ruth St. Denis whose influence has been greater than anyone else, especially in America, from various notions of Greek dancing, never possible as a school as long as we are ignorant of Greek music, and more recently from Central Europe. Whatever their claims, they are neither revolutionary nor even novel in their results. They can be and often are artistically satisfying.

The technique of classical ballet, properly understood, embraces every type of movement; rigid, supple and acrobatic.

Notice the back bends in the final waltz of *Les Sylphides* or of the odalisques in *Schéhérazade*, the astonishing leaps and falls in *The Blue Train*, the frenzied jazz in *Beach*, the can-can in *La Boutique Fantasque*, Massine's barman's dance in *Union Pacific*, the turned in movements *en profile* in *L'Après-midi*

d'un Faune, the turned out movements in *Aurora's
Wedding,* the Rumba in *Jardin Public,* the leaps in
Prince Igor, the different quality leap in *Le Spectre de
la Rose,* the Spanish rhythmic heel movements in *Le
Chapeau Tricorne,* most popular ballet in Spain itself,
the Lesginka, traditional Cossack dance in *Thamar.*
All these have been achieved by dancers trained in
the same manner. Facts such as these alone count.
They prove conclusively that the ballet-trained
dancer can with a few rehearsals perform whatever
the 'free' dancer can, while the reverse is not the case.

The 'free' dancer is not in fact free, but is physically
limited in what she can express.

*Classical ballet is not an end in itself. It is but a means
to an almost unlimited number of ends.*

With the classical system of training and the
Fokine conception of choreography, every end in
dancing can be attained.

In many discussions with exponents of free dancing I have felt myself in entire sympathy with their
aims, often partially with the results. Where we have
disagreed has been in their methods.

To take an example from everyday life: there is
nothing to prevent the highly trained surgeon or
physician from practising osteopathy. Osteopathy

may cure certain conditions, but why rely exclusively on a more limited method when the larger and more comprehensive one exists?

The dancer has been very largely to blame in any misunderstanding of ballet. The 'free' dancer has generally studied music more carefully and has investigated movement for herself, rather than accepting a whole system without investigation. The education of the ballet dancer should include a more general artistic outlook. In Russia it was both more leisurely and more comprehensive.

Outside the ballet tradition the one man who has created important original work is Kurt Jooss, a choreographer of strong musical knowledge and real imagination. He seems to me to have gained nothing through being outside the tradition. He has limited the vocabulary which he might use. His choreography is rich in literary idea, rich in pattern and singularly poor in actual dancing steps. His most brilliant episode is the group of diplomats, round the green table, which by its very nature does not require much dancing. It is an effect that cannot be often repeated. In his work as a whole he uses much that is balletic, including the *entrechat*,[1] and

[1] See page 111.

his work could not exist without the ballet technique. Then suddenly he stops short and avoids taking the final plunge. His reason is certainly not a latent dilettantism and his dancers are marvellously disci, plined and very highly trained in the abbreviated technique.

This poverty of step, moreover, throws great onus on his imagination. If the situation he is illus, trating is not strongly dramatic, if his inspiration nods for a moment, then there is failure, without the standby of interesting an audience with complex movement for its own sake.

Compare Death in *The Green Table* and Fate in *Les Présages*, two very similar conceptions. Both are fairly banal conventional ideas, both effective from a dramatic viewpoint. Once the first shock of Death has communicated itself to the audience there is little left; Fate, on the other hand, without being the greater dramatic creation, has still many surprises in pure dancing.

Death's protagonists react in a very similar manner, run or are attracted; Fate's protagonists can show fear and triumph in an endless variety of movement, both on the point and off. In this particular Jooss ballet the point would be 'unrealistic', yet the point dancer has still infinitely greater possibilities of movement. Jooss excels in political satire. It is a new field for ballet, but it is no more revolutionary than any of the importations of Massine or Nijinska. It is significant that his new productions have carried him no further than *The Green Table* and those smaller exquisite productions, *A Ball in Old Vienna* and *The Pavane.*

In *A Ball in Old Vienna* by avoiding points he has preserved the true waltz style, and the work is a rich compound of Viennese, German and Russian waltz movement, but an orthodox choreographer might equally well have kept his dancers off their points and a ballet company could certainly have performed it. Massine's waltzes and mazurka in *Beau Danube* are stylised, Vienna translated into Ballet. Jooss' are the actual things themselves.

This is not special pleading in favour of ballet, it is the logical conclusion of this section devoted to choreography, the aim of which has been to show the infinite possibilities that the Fokine use of an old established art possesses, and the impossibility of revolting from it, once it is clearly understood.

XVII

THE DANCER AS AN ARTIST—BIRTH
OF THE SYLPHIDE

WE have given our dancer, Mary, a long wait while we have been examining the exact nature of her work, and however ideal the conditions under which it is composed, it depends upon her finally to convey its meaning to the public. She is the contact between the auditorium and the colla⁄ borators' studio, a person of considerable import⁄ ance, for it lies with her to save a bad work or mar a good one.

She is presumed, now she has joined a company, to be mechanically and technically efficient. I use two words here to indicate different things; by the first I mean simply the ability to execute movements, by the second the ability to present those movements effectively.

An important point to decide is how far she is an executive artist and how far free and creative. Clearly in movement she must follow the choreography without distortion, but that still leaves her an enormous field for exercising her own personality. I can think of two striking examples where dancers built up important rôles from very slender material. Lydia Sokolova in *Les Matelots* created a comic part that has died completely without her, Irina Baronova developed the soubrette in *Le Beau Danube* into something irresistibly charming and personal.

It is of course easier to do this in the modern, non-romantic ballet, where a rôle is a far more positive thing. Is it possible to show individuality in *Les Sylphides*? Undoubtedly, by the very nature of our art. The dancer has her set steps, but her guide as to interpretation as well as tempo comes from the orchestra. In no two people can music provoke identical reactions. In the majority of dancers the music provokes no reaction at all, with the consequence that they have nothing to give the audience but a series of steps. In a good ballet, steps should be entirely forgotten. Also, it is not enough for the dancer to have a sound musical ear. To move her audience she must herself be moved.

Watching this same *Sylphides* my neighbour says, 'Look at that girl, third on the left, she's the most graceful of the lot. She's got them all beat.' I turn round and say 'Hush', but follow him out in the interval to ask why. He is perfectly right, everyone has noticed it, but all find it impossible to say more than, 'Well, graceful, you know what that means'. 'Do you mean light?' 'Perhaps a little, though that skinny girl on the left is very much lighter—I mean graceful—you know what I mean.'

Actually this is an extremely difficult quality to define, this thing that singles out one girl from a crowd. It is something fundamental that none can express and everyone can feel. I am not referring here to the intangible 'personality', but to a very definite dancing quality, something so physically real that one can say in truth that many 'dancers', even famous ones, cannot really dance at all. They can perform steps brilliantly, but their work never flows. It is made up of a series of little joins. It is staccato, and that sometimes gives a spurious brilliance.

What does the popular phrase 'meaningless arms' convey when applied to a dance that has no meaning that can be put into words? It conveys just that lack of a true dance conception, arms that are *obviously* preparing the dancer for the next movement and that are out of the picture of the dance as a whole.

Fluidity and large movements whose line can be extended indefinitely are the essential characteristics of the Russian School.

In a recent film of Anna Pavlova, *Rondino* in slow motion, I could analyse this quality that has always been described as her 'indefinable magic'. It is the *oneness* of her dancing that makes it like something in Nature, a gentle ripple on a pond, the gradual unfolding of a flower. It is more than a physical gift, it comes from my first point, a strong musical reaction. That is one of the distinguishing marks between dancing, even virtuoso dancing and acrobacy, one of the factors that makes Lifar's suggested relationship between music and dancing a false one.

This true dance conception is often something inborn. I have noticed it in young pupils, whose technical repertoire was very restricted, yet whose work gave one an immense satisfaction. It can be developed, but I doubt very much if it can ever be learned.[1] The education of the ballet public can best

---

[1] This gift is strongly marked among certain of the younger dancers, in the Russians Irina Baronova and Tamara Toumanova, in our own astonishing Margot Fonteyn and in the American Ruth Chanova. Impossible to compare them on other grounds; it is something positive that they have in common.

develop it. Unfortunately, *applause is usually the reaction to a realisation of difficulty overcome, and not to beauty understood.*

Another reason that will cause my neighbour to pick out one girl from a group and ask her name is personality. It is positive, more recognisable than artistry or technical ability, but it cannot be defined. It does not consist in drawing attention to oneself by anything deliberate. Its presence will make one over-praise the indifferent dancer, its absence ignore so much fine work. If our dancer Mary lacks it, she must be prepared to remain in the *corps de ballet* for the rest of her life. She will be praised, called a 'useful' dancer, deputise for each *première danseuse* in turn and never retain the rôles. A sad fate!

But with the true dance conception and person-ality she can conquer the world.

For me personally it counts above all else. I can enjoy the per-formance of a pupil with it, dislike a highly accomplished *ballerina* who lacks it—and it *is* rare.

XVIII

TYPES OF DANCER

I T is the ambition of every dancer to be a *prima ballerina*, the first in a company as exponent of the 'ballet blanc', *Swan Lake* and *Aurora*, and of the neo-classics such as *Les Sylphides*. However talented the dancer this is not always possible of attainment. It must be clearly understood that there are categories of dancers just as there are sopranos, mezzo-sopranos and contraltos amongst singers. With the dancer just as with the singer the differences are firstly physical. The classical *ballerina* needs a certain type of physique, not too great height, legs that are perfect in formation, for they will show the entire time under the short 'tutu'.

The differences between the types are also psycho-logical. The classical dancer may possess enormous temperament, but it must be held severely in check or the result will be vulgar. Classicism demands intense self-discipline.

87

In practice, therefore, between the physical and psychological difficulties, but few are suited to be *ballerinas*. The advantage of the *ballerina* is that with her discipline she usually possesses an enormous range and can encroach on the other categories with ease. Karsavina was as famous for her classical dancing as her character and *demi-caractère*, Pavlova could perform *Giselle*, a Bacchanal and a Mexican dance in the same programme, and to-day those two outstanding *ballerinas* Baronova and Toumanova are at home in every type of work.

The nearest approach to the purely classical is *demi-caractère*, which combines classical ballet technique with a part to create. A typical example of this is Columbine in *Carnaval*, dancing on the points combined with a difficult problem in mime.

Although this is a definite division, in one sense all great dancing is *demi-caractère*, since there is always a problem in mime, even if there is no positive character to create. In purely classical work the dancer may be said to be acting herself, re-creating her character for the stage. That is why many dancers who are reserved by nature succeed better when there is a rôle behind which to conceal themselves, even when from a physical point of view they may appear to be perfect classical dancers. The good *maître de ballet* needs to be a practical psychologist in his casting.

The third category is that of character dancing, under which may be included both national dancing —*Le Tricorne*, *Prince Igor*—and such mimed rôles as Zobeide in *Schéhérazade* and *Thamar*.

XIX

THE MALE DANCER

U P to this point I have referred to the dancer in the feminine, and were this written in Paris about the year 1900 it would have sufficed, for in Western Europe in general the male dancer was almost extinct, the *porteur* alone existed.

All the basic remarks I have made about Mary's dancing apply equally well to John's, but there are some further points to be considered.

The male dancer is used not merely to lift, but to enrich the orchestration of dancing by forming a contrast to the woman.

It follows that *the effeminate male dancer is without exception a bad dancer.*

Also it is well to stress the fact that grace and virility are not incompatible and that the male *premier danseur classique* can be as masculine as the male character dancer, if he understands his function.

It is in *The Swan Lake* that we can see the basis of

his function the most clearly, for here he is not yet
fully a dancer in his own right. In such a classical
ballet he is the intermediary between the *ballerina* and
the public, by his whole manner he draws attention
to her presence. A good male classical dancer can
double the *ballerina's* applause by his chivalry. His
whole attitude is that of a man thinking: 'Look at
her, how light she is. I am not lifting this ethereal
creature, she floats. She weighs nothing at all.'
When she dances he must stand motionless, his eyes
fixed delightedly upon her. This technique is ex⁄
tremely elaborate and can most certainly be learned
by any dancer down to its smallest detail. The lack
of it makes the average man who dances the Prince
look completely lost, which in fact he is, for he is
standing on the stage completely without any *raison
d'être*.[1] The whole composition of these classical
ballets demands male awe and chivalry. The *ballerina*
is invariably some enchanted being; a Bluebird
dancing with a Prince, a Wraith, a Swan.

In *Les Sylphides* he comes into his own as a dancer.
What a touch of genius to put him there, the solitary

---

[1] Of the younger dancers Robert Helpmann is almost alone
in being convincing in this rôle, though his classical technique
is limited.

man, in spite of what a provincial theatre manager in America said to Colonel de Basil, 'I like the ballet very much, it's dainty, but what's that guy doing there all by himself? I'd get rid of him.'

His being there adds to the ballet in a number of ways, apart from the obvious one of his lifting; in the first function mentioned of admirer, in giving a contrast between male and female technique, in giving a psychological contrast, a much sublimated love interest that is nevertheless very definite. In the *Spectre de la Rose* the man is essential, and a male rose is not effeminate, he is the gentle lover of whom the maiden dreams.

I must admit that in practice the majority of male dancers to-day are effeminate, because the majority are frankly bad. They damage the whole structure of ballet as a consequence. The normal audience re-action is, 'I like the women, but it's not a man's job to dance'. Such a reaction is never produced in the normal person by first-class male dancing in spite of black velvet jacket and flowing locks, a romantic costume no more effeminate than the silks, satins and curls worn by so doughty a swordsman as Athos.

XX

BALLET: THE FUTURE

W E have now returned to a period of technical virtuosity, in which the choreographers' scope is enormous.

The history of the *fouetté*,[1] so much in vogue to-day, is but one illustration of that.

Perfected by the Italian dancer Legnani and used by her in *The Swan Lake*, it caused a sensation, the audience counting aloud as she performed her famous 32. It was considered by the best writers an unworthy acrobatic trick, and it did not catch on generally, though the great *ballerina* Kchesinska learnt and mastered it. Valerian Svetloff, writing in about 1910, said: 'If 32 *fouettés*, why not 42, 52 and 80, on to infinity, resulting in the complete mechanisation of the dance. Technique must go no further.'

For a time technique was in advance of choreography. It became still more so. With the further

[1] See page 111.

perfection of teaching, small children learned to perform 50, 60, 70, an endless series of *fouettés*, learned to perform them with grace and ease.[1] Then choreography caught up and began to use them, not as acrobatics but to express some definite emotion, with dramatic justification; gaiety in *Le Beau Danube*, the spinning of the top in *Jeux d'Enfants*.

In view of this it is not possible to consider tech‚ nique as stationary. It will surely continue to develop. Of late the whole general level of dancing has improved, technically again rather than artistically. The individual is gradually ceding place to the group of talented individuals, the very young and immature personality replacing the dominating figure. It is an age of *premières danseuses* rather than *prima ballerinas*. This, again, gives more scope to the choreographer who can create his dancers for his rôles.

Where ballet is declining, let us hope temporarily, is in the close collaboration of music and décor. The

[1] Tamara Toumanova was the first to inaugurate the modern *fouetté* period and the three rôles that caused a sensation; *Cotillon*, *Concurrence* and *Jeux d'Enfants* were created by her. She was speedily followed by Irina Baronova, from the same studio, that of Olga Preobrajenska.

dance has forged ahead, leaving its partners behind.

The most encouraging sign of all is the establish⁄ment of permanent schools in England—Sadler's Wells and the Ballet Club, and in America—American National Ballet and Metropolitan Opera. This, taken in conjunction with the fine achievement of the de Basil Russian Ballet, only inheritor of the great Russian tradition in Western Europe and to whom this fertile state is largely due, should assure the future of ballet.

CHRONOLOGICAL SUMMARY

GLOSSARY · APPENDIX · INDEX

A BRIEF CHRONOLOGICAL
SUMMARY OF BALLET HISTORY

1661. Louis XIV, the first ballet dancer, establishes L'Académie Royale de la Danse.

Only twenty years later did women make an appearance in ballet, appropriately enough in Lully's *Le Triomphe de L'Amour*. These first dancers were such ladies of the court as Mlle de Poitiers and Madame de Sévigné.

1721. From the first appearance of La Camargo modern ballet is conceived, the professional dancer superseding the dilettante. By shortening the costume but a few inches, through which she scandalised many, and thus giving liberty to the feet, the dance was free to develop on virtuoso lines. The graceful amateur was now left far behind. Sallé, Camargo's great rival, was the first to wear a Greek tunic on the stage as Galatea in a ballet *Pygmalion* danced at Covent Garden.

The whole history of the development of ballet technique is closely bound up with the history of costume, for instance with the shortening of the skirt, Camargo knew the beginnings of the *entrechat*.

In these early days, when technique developed so rapidly, *maîtres de ballets* were especially interested in the development of footwork, often at the expense of the body as a whole.

1735. The Empress Anne founds a ballet school in Russia. Many great nobles and landowners already possessed their own troupes of serf actors and dancers.

1759. Noverre, the great *maître de ballet* admired of Voltaire, begins his letters, laying down the principles of ballet which remain unchanged to-day, and attacking the abuses which were already strangling the art. (See text, page 37.) Born in 1727 of Swiss origin, Noverre became *maître de ballet* of the Opéra Comique in 1747. So great was his renown that David Garrick called him to Drury Lane. Disappointed in his wish to enter the Grand Opera, in spite of the intervention of Madame de Pompadour, he spread his knowledge of the art in Württemberg, Vienna, Milan and throughout Italy. In Vienna he became the teacher of Marie Antoinette, who opened for him the doors of the Grand Opera. The revolution made him an exile once again and he mounted his last work in London on the day of Louis XVI's murder.

1766. Mlle Heinel of Stuttgart performs an amazing step in Paris—the *pirouette*.

1801. Didelot, a great French *maître de ballet*, arrives in St. Petersburg. By fostering native talent he commences the great Russian tradition. Already the Russian Istomina, made immortal by Pushkin, is a great *ballerina*. Other French *maîtres de ballets* follow him. St. Petersburg begins to count as an important dance centre.

An important development of costume affecting the dance is the invention of tights by Maillot, costumier of the Paris Opera.

1820. Carlo Blasis publishes his famous treatise on the dance, codifying all that is known of its technique. This volume was written when he was seventeen years of age. It renders homage

to Noverre as an aesthetician, though it
declares that so great and rapid has been the
technical development of ballet that those portions of his work are now out of date. Blasis
stresses the value of the feet being turned out at
an angle of ninety degrees, basis of classicism.

He founded the famous academy of dancing in Milan, second only in importance to
that in Paris, and for half a century his word
was law.

1821. Debut of La Taglioni and the beginnings of
the great romantic movement.

Eugene Lamy's costume design for her
great success *La Sylphide,* with but little
modification, is the tarlatan dress we know so
well to-day. Costume has progressed from the
heaviness of court dress to the professional attire
of to-day.

This is the golden age of Cerrito, Ellssler,
Grahn and Grisi. So great is their success that
the male dancer plays from now on an entirely
subordinate position, only to come into his
own again with Fokine and Nijinsky. (See
text, page 90.)

1841. Carlotta Grisi creates the rôle of Giselle in

Coralli's ballet, the oldest to survive in the
repertoire, unaltered in essentials from that day
till the present. (See text, page 40.)

1847. Marius Petipa arrives in Russia as a dancer
and eleven years later is appointed *maître de
ballet*.

1862. He produces a sensational five-act ballet *La
Fille de Pharaon*. Under his regime, lasting
fifty years, during which he composed over
sixty full-length ballets, technique and the
virtuoso side of ballet is enormously developed
(See text, page 41.)

Some twenty years later the arrival in St.
Petersburg of Enrico Cecchetti, inheritor from
Giovanni Lepri of the Italian tradition,
develops the school still further and makes of
it what we know to-day, the perfect blend of
French and Italian methods.

1890 (*circa*). Tchaikovsky collaborates with Petipa,
setting an example to other serious composers.
He is followed by Glazounov in *Raymonda*.
(See text, page 41.)

1905. Fokine arranges *The Swan*, beginning of a
new aesthetic. (See text, page 43.)

1907. Isadora Duncan dances in St. Petersburg.

Production of the Benois-Fokine *Pavillon d'Armide*, transition between the old and the new. An event of extraordinary importance, for it is now that the artistic group controlled by Diaghileff and Benois began to use ballet as their medium, so giving it a new life. (See text, page 56.)

1908. With Fokine's *Eunice*, Greek tunic is worn for the first time in ballet on the Maryinsky stage. (See text, page 48.)

1909. Diaghileff ballet debut in Paris. Especial success of *Prince Igor*. The male dancer regains his status. (See text, page 90.)

1910. The first important commissioned music for ballet, Stravinsky's *L'Oiseau de Feu*; the beginnings of a new direction in ballet music. (See text, page 34.)

Publication of Fokine's letter in *The Times*. (See text, page 45.)

Pavlova comes to London and begins the Russian Invasion.

1911. Diaghileff London debut.

1912/13. Nijinsky's ballets *L'Après-midi d'un Faune* and *Le Sacre du Printemps* cause a sensation. (See text, page 66.)

1915. Massine begins his career as choreographer with *Le Soleil de Nuit,* and from this date to the present day follow an amazing sequence of important works. (See text, page 67.)

1921. Nijinska begins choreography for Diaghileff.

1924. Serge Lifar joins the Russian Ballet.

1925. Balanchine begins choreography for Diaghileff. (See text, page 69.)

Olga Preobrajenska opens a studio in Paris, later to be followed by Vera Trefilova, Mathilde Kchesinska and Lubov Egorova.

1929. Death of Serge Diaghileff.

1930. Formation of Camargo Society, London.

1931. Death of Anna Pavlova.

Ballet Club and Vic-Wells Ballet formed in London.

1932. Formation of Col. W. de Basil's Ballets Russes de Monte Carlo.

1933. London premières of first symphonic ballets *Les Présages* and *Choreartium* (see text, page 67), and

Formation of Balanchine's American Ballet, New York.

1935. *In England:*

Eight ballet companies appear in London;[1] seven of them perform *Les Sylphides*, five *Carnaval*, four *Le Spectre de la Rose*. Two of the companies have permanent London homes, Marie Rambert's Ballet Club and The Vic-Wells.

In America:

Enormous success of the de Basil tour. Debut of Balanchine's American Ball. Reform of the Metropolitan Ballet under Balanchine.

1936. New productions at Sadler's Wells; *Baiser de la Fée* (Stravinsky–Ashton), *Apparitions* (Liszt–Ashton), *The Gods go a-begging* (Handel–de Valois, *Barabau* (Rieti–de Valois) and many revivals revealing the talent of Margot Fonteyn, Elizabeth Miller and other young dancers developed in the company as well as the more experienced Pearl Argyle, Ursula Moreton, Robert Helpmann and Harold Turner. The first big season creatively for a national ballet in England.

[1] Marie Rambert, Lithuanian, Vic-Wells, de Basil Ballet Russe, Ballet Russe de Paris, Leon Woizikovski, Ballet Jooss, Markova-Dolin.

GLOSSARY OF TECHNICAL AND SEMI-TECHNICAL TERMS

I T is impossible to explain the technique of ballet adequately in print. The many excellent technical books that exist are for the use of the dancer already familiar with the terms in practice. Certain terms, however, need explanation in order to make any writing on ballet understandable. I am treating them here not in strict alphabetical order, but in logical sequence, not in technical phraseology, but in the simplest fashion possible so that they are approxima-tions intended to aid the amateur in identifying steps.

Dancing is an art built up around an exact science of movement. Our concern is with the art. Both the experienced dancer and the *balletomane* must learn to think of dancing as a whole and not of isolated steps.

CLASSICAL BALLET

In time this means the pre-Fokine ballets that still

survive in the repertoire; Giselle, Coppelia, the works of Marius Petipa. It must never be confused with attempts at reviving the Greek dance. Its aesthetics I have already discussed. Classical ballet is sometimes called after its costume, *ballet blanc*.

While there are many systems of ballet, basically they are identical, and the universal language is that of the country of origin, France.

The classical system is built around the five positions of the feet and variations on those positions.

The Five Positions of the Feet

(1) Heels touching, feet in a line forming an angle of 90°.

(2) The same line with a distance of one foot between the heels.

(3) One foot in front of the other, one heel touching the middle of the other.

(4) The same. The feet parallel, with one foot distance between them.

(5) Feet closed. Parallel. The heel of one foot touching the toe joint of the other.

These positions are susceptible to variation; on the ground (*à terre*), in the air (*en l'air*), *demi-position*, etc.

There are also various movements of the feet; *à terre*, *à quart* (heel slightly raised), *sur la demi-pointe* (foot supported on ball of toes), *à trois quarts*, *sur la pointe* (see text, page 8, for solemn warning).

CARRIAGE OF THE ARMS, ETC.

The most difficult question in dancing is the *port de bras*, in which there are corresponding positions to the feet. It is in the arm positions that the dancer can show true beauty of line. Dancing does not cease at the wrist; there are also positions of the hands. The head, too, has its five positions, vital in such steps as *pirouettes*, where it should be the last to move when the body turns away from the spectator, the first to move when it returns. The body, too, has careful rules for its carriage and eight different directions for movement.

All these factors combined may seem extra-ordinarily complicated; they allow for every type of movement, but since they are based on natural laws the complication is more on paper than in practice.

MOVEMENTS IN DANCING

There are seven categories of movement in dancing: *Plier* (to bend), *Étendre* (to stretch), *Relever* (to raise), *Glisser* (to slide), *Sauter* (to jump), *Élancer* (to dart), *Tourner* (to turn).

. . . .

ADAGIO.—The 'high spot' of classical ballet. The dance in which the ballerina, assisted by her male partner, reveals her virtuosity.

ARABESQUE.—There are a variety of arabesques. Basically it indicates the position of the body on one leg with the other leg extended behind, one arm extended in front of the body, the other behind. It forms the longest line that can be made from finger tips to toes.

ATTITUDE.—Another position of great beauty, based by Carlo Blasis on Jan Bologna's Mercury. The Maître de ballet in taking the rôle of Mercury concluded a pirouette in this position.

There are an indefinite number of possible *attitudes*. Basically it is a pose in which the body is supported on one foot, with the other raised and the knee bent. The arms are rounded and the body curved backwards.

BALLON.—Referring not to the height of a jump but to the correct manner of landing in order to take off again (*i.e.* bounce).

BARRE.—The wooden railing running along the walls of a dance studio as a support during exercise.

ELEVATION.—The opposite of *terre à terre*. Dancing off the ground.

ENCHAÎNEMENT.—A sequence of steps. Where the step is a word this is a phrase.

ENTRECHAT.—A jump during which the feet change their position with regard to one another, from back to front and vice versa, four, six or eight times, quite exceptionally ten: *entrechats quatre, six,* etc. A twinkling movement depending on elevation and ballon.

FOUETTÉ.—Used unqualified this means a turn on one leg, accompanied by a whipping movement of the other, the working leg.

PAS DE BOURRÉE.—Progression on the points by a sequence of very small, even steps.

PIROUETTE.—A complete turn of the body, accomplished on one leg. A complete aerial turn is called a *tour en l'air.*

APPENDIX

A NOTE ON M. DOBOUJINSKY, DECORATOR OF THIS VOLUME

DOBOUJINSKY was one of that famous band of Russian artists grouped around Diaghileff's magazine, the *Mir Isskustva* (World of Art). Within ten years of its founding (1899) they had not only revolutionised the art of their own country in every branch, but had, through the medium of the ballet, completely revolutionised the whole decorative art of Western Europe. Their activities were confined to no one branch of art, and since the Italian Renaissance, perhaps no more cultured group of artists has existed than Benois, Bakst, Roerich, Serov, Somov and Doboujinsky.

For many years Bakst and Doboujinsky conducted an Academy of Art together in St. Petersburg, from which many famous painters emerged.

Doboujinsky is an outstanding example of the *Mir Isskustva* outlook; he truly covers a whole world

of art. To the theatre he has given a remarkabl
series of décors for Stanislavsky, Diaghileff an
other great producers.

He is a pioneer of Russian book illustration
which is second only in importance to Russia
theatrical art. This is the first English text to b
decorated by him.

INDEX

INDEX

Index

☙ *Index* ☙

THE END

THOMAS NELSON & SONS LTD

35-36 PATERNOSTER ROW, LONDON, E.C.4 ; PARKSIDE
WORKS, EDINBURGH ; 25 RUE DENFERT-ROCHEREAU,
PARIS ; 312 FLINDERS STREET, MELBOURNE ;
91-93 WELLINGTON STREET WEST, TORONTO ;
381-385 FOURTH AVENUE, NEW YORK

Printed in Great Britain at the press of the Publishers

The "Little Theatre" Series: Edited by John Hampden

PLAYS IN VERSE AND MIME

ROSALIND VALLANCE

'Lovely lines and movements, full of poetry and imagination.'—
Drama. 'The first book of a kind that we have been badly needing.
... The Narcissus play is quite perfect.'—GORDON BOTTOMLEY.
'We have nothing but praise for the plays which Miss Vallance
has given us.'—MARJORIE GULLAN: *Good Speech.* 'All these
plays are alive and vivid.'—*Amateur Theatre.*—Five plays of vary-
ing length and mood, for stage or lawn and for players young or
old. Full notes on acting, staging and gramophone music. Illus-
trations by C. Walter Hodges.   3*s.* 6*d.* net.

FIFTEEN MODERN PLAYS

Edited by JOHN HAMPDEN

'Another valuable collection.'—*Drama.* 'Selected by so experienced a connoisseur as Mr. Hampden this is a welcome volume
... especially as many of these plays are written for all-women or
all-men casts.'—One-act plays, ranging from farce to tragedy, by
Miles Malleson, Gordon Bottomley, Mary Kelly, Rosalind
Vallance, F. Sladen-Smith, Philip Johnson, etc. Full acting
notes.   3*s.* 6*d.* net.

JILL'S MAGIC ISLAND

AND OTHER STORIES FOR
CHILDREN'S BALLETS

by ERNEST A. JELF

Master of the Supreme Court

With 181 photographs of children in the plays

Jill's Magic Island—The Little Old Woman—The Cuckoo and the Cuckoo-flower—The Spartan Maid—The Baron's Enchanted Garden—Brenda and the Mice—Changes in the Weather—The Ghost of Columbine—The Blue Tit's Nest—The Country of 'Let's Pretend.'—An Epilogue.

These delightful stories are arranged as children's ballets founded on the works of Beethoven, Chopin, Grieg, etc. They offer opportunities for Greek dancing, operatic dancing, country dancing, minuets, valses, miming, and the simple 'skipping in time' of tiny children. The words can be read by one Reader, or divided to provide speaking parts. No acting fees. (Ages 5–18.)

Large quarto. Cloth gilt, 3s. 6d. net.

MIMES AND MIMING

by ISABEL CHISMAN *and* GLADYS WILES

A book for beginners as well as those who have already discovered the delights of miming. It shows *exactly* what to do, and besides chapters on miming it contains fourteen mimes, ranging from carols to farce, the casts of which can be easily increased or decreased if required. Stage plans, music, etc.

Carol: We Three Kings of Orient Are. *Simple Mimes with Chorus*: The Babes in the Wood. The Sleeping Beauty. *Songs and Folk-songs*: Billy Boy. The Wee Cooper o' Fife. The Wraggle-Taggle Gipsies, O. *Prose Mimes*: Gabriel Grub. The Swineherd. Bluebeard. The Jester. *Miscellaneous*: The Romantic Wooing. The Pest. *Ballads*: Sir Eglamore. Binnorie. No acting fees.

SECOND EDITION.   *Quarter cloth boards, 2s. 6d. net.*